STEP-BY-STEP
BEAD
STRINGING

A complete Illustrated Professional Approach.

BY RUTH F. PORIS
with drawings by the author

STEP-BY-STEP BEAD STRINGING

A complete Illustrated Professional Approach.

BY RUTH F. PORIS
with drawings by the author

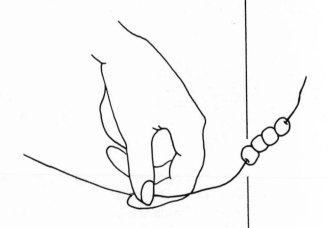

Golden Hands Press
Tampa, Florida

ISBN 0-9616422-1-1

15th Printing 1993
Copyright © 1984 by Ruth F. Poris
All Rights Reserved

Published by Golden Hands Press
4202 Water Oaks Lane
Tampa, Florida 33624
(813) 265-1681

Graphics by Brainstorm Design, Inc.
Ann Arbor, Michigan

Printed in U.S.A.

CONTENTS

"Charge all things you fashion with a breath of your own spirit"

— *Gibran*

INTRODUCTION

This handbook was written as a starting point for learning the basic skills of stringing and restringing beads. The instructions are fully illustrated and may be followed step by step. Once accomplished, bead stringing can be a very satisfying hobby or profitable business.

The instructions explain all basic techniques for working with beads, from simple inexpensive wood, plastic or glass, to precious gemstones and pearls. As in any craft, practice is the best guarantee of a beautiful product.

Use these instructions as a beginning, as there are no set rules to successful stringing. Experiment for yourself, working with size, color, textures and shapes. With imagination and the basic techniques contained in this book, the opportunity to produce original, well crafted, beaded jewelry is unlimited.

1 TOOLS AND SUPPLIES

Very simple equipment is needed for stringing. Having the proper supplies on hand makes the job much easier.

beading needles

Needles

Beading needles are made in various sizes and weights, to accommodate bead drill holes and thread. They are constructed of flexible, twisted wire, with a large hole which closes slightly when pulled through the drill hole. The most commonly used sizes are #6 (Fine), #10 (Medium) and #12 (Heavy). Size #10 is best for most pearls and small beads, while Size #12 is more suitable for larger, heavier beads. Some stringers prefer nylon cord with the needle permanently attached.

nylon with attached needle

This thread (with needle) is available in 16 weights in many colors. Some cord is stiff enough to use without a needle, others may be stiffened with glue or nail polish and twisted to form a pointed end.

Thread

Thread must be thin enough to pass through the drill holes, but strong enough to provide proper support for their weight. For medium to large beads, you can use upholstery or carpet thread. For small beads, buttonhole thread is satisfactory, although I recommend commercial beading thread.

upholstery or carpet cord

buttonhole twist

Pearl thread is available in thin, medium and heavy weight. Fishing line and "tigertail" (plastic coated wire) is also useful, although it cannot be knotted. "Tigertail" is available in 3 weights: thin (.012), medium (.018) and heavy (.021).

tigertail

For cultured pearls I recommend silk thread, as it knots very well, stretches less, and provides a soft, supple finish. Available in weights, 00 (thinnest) to FFF (heaviest), I suggest starting with sizes: #A and #D for very small pearls and #E and #FF for larger pearls and beads. Silk is available in 24 colors.

⅔ oz. silk

For really large beads, you can effectively use leather, yarn, rayon rattail, soutache or combinations of different weights and textures, for strength, as well as design.

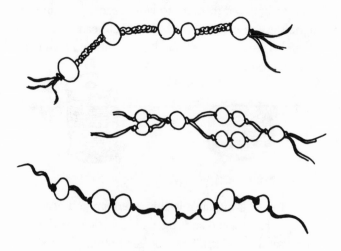

using cords for design and decorations

Bead Tips and Crimps

Bead tips come in two sizes: small and large. Small size is for thin to medium thread, large size for heavier cord. The most commonly used tips are gold or silver plated, but they are also available in 14 K yellow/white, goldfilled and sterling.

bead tip

Crimps are made in gold and silver color, in a number of styles. The tube crimp flattens to a rectangle and the narrow ring crimp to a narrow vertical band.

tube crimp

round crimp

Fasteners and Findings

Clasps are available in almost endless variety. They are made for single or multiple styles and in many kinds of metal.

filigree fishhook *smooth fishhook* *easy-lock clasp*

ball safety clasp *spring ring* *lobster*

double clasp *triple clasp*

Along with a starting supply of clasps, a small assortment of jump rings and split rings should be on hand.

jump ring *split ring*

Miscellaneous Needs

Glue Clear nail polish, colorless glue (Elmer's) or jeweler's crystal cement is needed at the end, where a small amount in the knot prevents unraveling. (I prefer crystal cement).

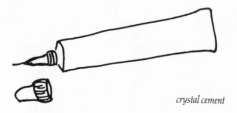

crystal cement

Scissors A good pair of embroidery scissors is useful for cutting thread. For cutting close to the beads, or taking apart a knotted strand. I suggest a pair of cuticle scissors or nippers.

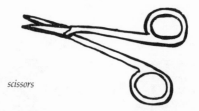

scissors

Ruler Two flat rulers are needed. For bracelets and chokers, have an 18" ruler on hand. For longer necklaces, a yardstick (36") is efficient. Since beads and pearls are calibrated in millimeters, a small millimeter gauge is also handy to own.

sliding gauge

Wax A small piece of beeswax (or a paraffin candle) strengthens the cord and prevents tangling. To wax the thread, just pull it gently over the wax.

Pliers Three pair of pliers are recommended: a small chain nose plier opens and closes bead tips, crimps and jump rings, and a small round nose plier is handy for bending round wire and bead tips. The small round nose is also useful for opening knots, without tearing the cord. Flat nose pliers have smooth jaws for holding flat or square objects firmly.

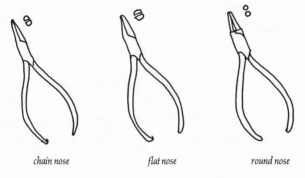

chain nose   *flat nose*   *round nose*

Workspace Any flat surface, from desk to tabletop is adequate. A large piece of felt or soft fabric (like velvet) is needed to prevent the beads from rolling. A handy, portable bead table may be constructed from an 18" square of wood, with fabric stretched over the surface and taped to the back.

adjustable lamp

Light Good lighting prevents eyestrain and is probably the most important piece of equipment. Your eyes will tell you when light is inadequate!

Optional Equipment Tweezers and a small spoon are handy for sorting and picking up beads. For storage, plastic compartment boxes become necessary when jars and cans are outgrown.

tweezer

plastic compartment box

A professional bead board is quite helpful for laying out patterns and graduated beads. A small pin vise, with size 70 and 75 drill bits is good for pushing old cord from drill holes. Sometimes a straight pin will be adequate.

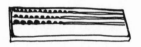

bead stringing board

pin vise

Helpful Suggestions

1. Sit at a comfortable height with good light and an uncluttered surface.

2. Lay out all the beads and equipment you need for the job within easy reach.

3. Before restringing, clean beads and cultured pearls by immersing them for a few minutes in a tepid solution of mild Ivory or Lux and water. Gently scrub with a soft brush, or sponge. Rinse thoroughly with warm water and pat dry with a soft cloth or towel. Handle the strand carefully, as the thread may be worn and can easily break when wet. To remove glue from gemstone or cultured pearls, soak them in a product called "Attack" for about an hour. Rinse them thoroughly, then push out the old cord with pin vise, or needle.

4. When cutting apart a necklace, do it over a tray or dish to prevent loss. If the design is patterned or graduated, carefully place each bead on the work surface, to maintain original design.

5. Masking tape is handy for laying out a pattern (on the tape), as well as picking up spilled beads and small thread scraps from the work table.

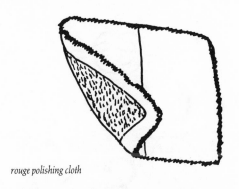

rouge polishing cloth

6. A Rouge Polishing Cloth is helpful for shining clasps and beads that have dimmed from use or handling.

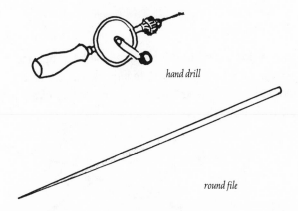

hand drill

round file

7. Having a hand drill is not necessary, but very helpful. An awl, for knotting, and small round file (needle file) is also good to own.

2 PLAIN STRINGING AND RESTRINGING

Plain stringing is the term used to describe beads strung on cord, without knots between them. My own technique includes knotting the first two beads at each end (for strength). Two simple knots are used. Practice both before stringing your beads.

overhand knot

make loop, pull cord through

Square Knot—used to double knot the bead tip, and in finishing a continuous (or endless) necklace. Make an overhand knot with left thread, then another overhand knot with right thread.

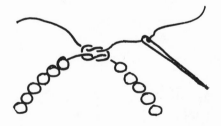

square knot closure

Single Strand

1. Remove old cord if restringing. If cord is stuck inside bead, use a straight pin or tiny drill to push it out.

2. Arrange the beads on your work table as you wish them to appear on the finished piece. Lay out all materials needed: beadtips, thread, wax, scissors, clasp, glue. Measure your cord, adding approximately ten inches to the (finished) length of the necklace.

single strand

3. Uniform beads (one size) should have the best in the center front, with lesser quality at the back, near the clasp.

4. If the necklace is graduated, the largest bead should be in the center, with an even number of beads on each side.

graduated necklace

5. Using the largest cord that will pass through the bead holes, pass the thread through the bead tip hole, (facing cup) and make an overhand knot. Make two square knots on top of overhand, and cut the thread as close as possible. Pull the thread, forcing the knot into the bead tip cup.

bead tip with knot

Dab glue or clear nail polish on the knot, and close the bead tip onto the clasp with the chain nose plier.

6. Thread 1st bead on, close to the tip. Make an overhand knot.

7. Thread 2nd bead on, make another overhand knot.

8. String each bead onto thread, until all but last three are placed according to pattern.

9. Make overhand knot; string next bead. Make 2nd overhand knot and string last bead. *Do not tie a knot after the last bead.*

10. Push the needle and thread through the 2nd bead tip, with hole facing the beads.

11. Make overhand, or square knot and slide it into the cup (takes practice!). Then make one or two more knots over the first one, so that it is secure and tight inside the cup. Cut the thread close and apply a generous dab of glue to the knot.

12. Attach bead tip to clasp and close with plier.

combining size, shape and materials

Multiple Strand or "Bib"

double strand bracelet

1. Lay out one strand at a time, starting with the longest.

2. As you add on the shorter lengths, remember that the beads must not touch the strand below. Measure each length as you go along, allowing ½" (for very small beads) to 3" (for larger beads).

3. Clasps are available with varied numbers of ring ends for 2/3/4/5 etc. strands.

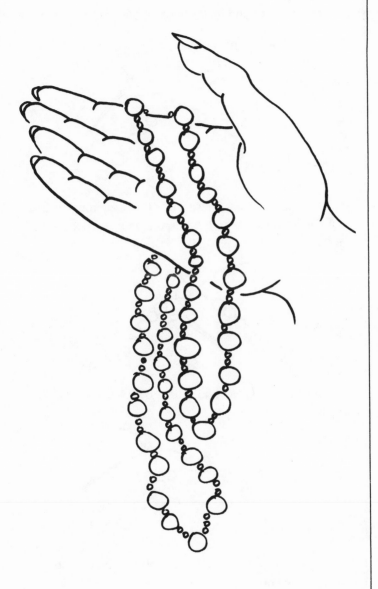

For necklaces long enough to slip over the head (26″ or more) the clasp may be omitted, and a knotted closure used.

1. Cut doubled cord long enough to leave 10″ at each side of finished length of necklace.

2. Thread needle and make an overhand knot at the end.

3. String all beads onto cord.

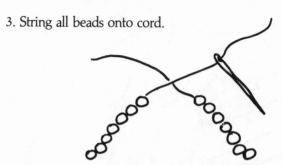

4. When all the beads are strung on, arrange them so that both ends of cord have 10″ to spare. Holding both ends of the cord up will shift all the beads to the center.

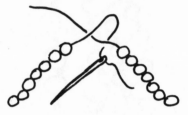

5. Tie cord in a square knot (Right over left, left over right)

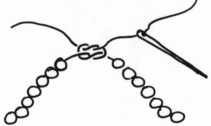

6. Leaving a slight space between the two beads, dab glue on the knot.

7. Push the needle and thread back through three beads, knotting between each bead, then thread without knots through the next two or three beads. Cut the cord, close and glue.

8. Repeat on other side.

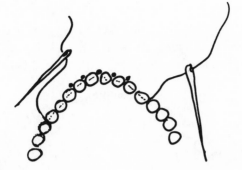

9. When using this closure, try to reserve the beads with largest holes for ending. Wax the thread thoroughly to help ease it back through holes. Sometimes it is necessary to pass one single thread at a time through the beads.

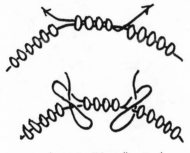

alternate tie off for endless strand

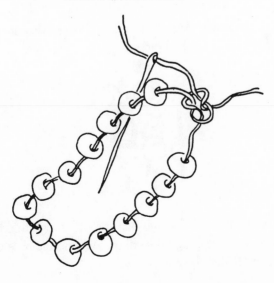

Tigertail Wire

Tigertail (nylon fused on wire) is the easiest and fastest method of stringing. As it tends to kink, be careful to avoid bending or folding the wire. It should not be knotted.

graduated necklace on tigertail

1. Lay out beads, clasp, 2 crimps, and wire. Measure wire 6" longer than finished piece.

2. Thread the wire through one crimp, through the clasp ring, and back through the crimp. With needle nose or flat plier, flatten the crimp.

3. String on all beads, then the 2nd crimp. Thread wire through second clasp ring, then back through crimp, keeping as close to clasp as possible. Flatten 2nd crimp.

4. No needle is required, so the design can be started in the center, adding beads to each side.

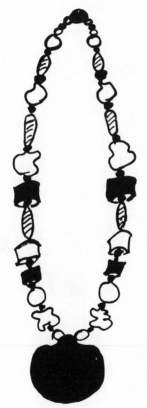

pendant with pattern design on tigertail

5. Monofilament (fishing line) can be used the same way, although it is better to use fishing line in double thickness. To secure the endings when using monofilament, touch a lighted match to the end, which will melt to a small bead.

3 KNOTTING BETWEEN BEADS

Knotting between each bead serves three purposes: it secures each bead against loss if the string breaks, it prevents pearls and fine beads from rubbing against each other and it provides an aesthetically pleasing design.

ivory and ebony with attached penda

Knotting requires great patience and practice to learn, but once achieved, the skill is well worth the effort! As a number of techniques can be used, experiment until you find the most satisfactory method for your needs.

Method A   (Knotting with thumb and forefinger)

1. Lay out beads as you do for plain stringing. Check to see that the cord is thick enough to fill the drill holes and that the knot will not slip through the hole.

2. Measure and cut a (doubled) length of cord, twice as long as the anticipated finished necklace. Mechanics are the same for single or doubled cord,

3. Tie a double knot, glue, and attach to bead tip.

4. Attach bead tip to clasp.

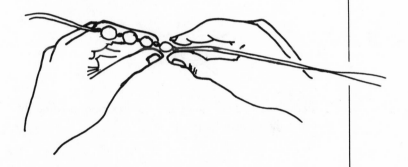

5. Thread 1st bead on and push up against bead tip. Tie a simple overhand knot, moving the knot tight against the bead. Push with thumb and forefinger. If doubled cord is used, separate the cords and pull the knot up tight to the bead. (This step requires practice!)

6. Continue knotting until the end. Finish off as in plain stringing. Remember not to knot after the last bead.

Method B   (Knotting with Tweezer or Awl)

Follow steps 1–4 as in Method A.

5. Thread on 1st bead and push against bead tip.

6. Make a large loop in thread about the size of a quarter

7. Place the tweezer or awl through the loop, holding the thread tight against the bead.

8. Ease the knot down toward the bead and over the tips of the tweezers, until it is tight.

9. Continue knotting until the end. Finish off as in plain stringing.

Double Knotting

This is an added technique which is very useful to learn.
Sometimes, when drill holes are very large, it is practical
to use double knots, although it is also quite attractive
when different color threads are combined. This skill is
definitely a design advantage, and worth practicing.

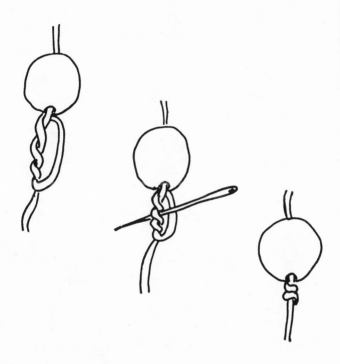

The double knot is easy to perfect, once the single knot
is mastered. They are almost exactly alike. Follow
the illustrations.

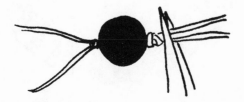

Helpful Suggestions

1. Before you begin, test two or three beads with a short length of cord. Make sure the knots will not slip through drill holes.

2. Remember that knotting extends the length of the necklace. Allow for 1"–3" added length, plus ½"–1" for the clasp.

3. Measure your cord carefully before you start. Very large beads and knots will sometimes require more cord than double the length of the finished piece.

4. Make the knots as tight as possible, as the weight of the beads will loosen them.

5. Cord can improve the design. Experiment with different colors, textures and sizes mixed together.

6. Practice before you begin any major job.

7. The finished length of a bracelet or necklace always includes the clasp.

triple collar with bone spacers, wood and silver

4 FINISHING WITH FRENCH WIRE

Using French Wire (Boullion) is the most professional way to finish beaded jewelry. Made of fine wire wound like a spring into a flexible, hollow tube, boullion is available in fine, medium, and heavy weights and in yellow or white wire. Approximately ¼"–½" is used for each end, to form proper size loops for your job.

french wire

1. Lay out beads, cord and clasp.

2. Choose boullion which will pass through the thread and clasp ring.

3. Cut 1" of Boullion (approximately ½" for each side).

4. Thread needle and knot end of cord with overhand knot, leaving 1–2" tail at end.

5. Thread three (3) end beads onto cord. Push up to knot.

6. Thread on (approx) ½" French Wire, push up to bead.

7. Loop the thread and French Wire through the clasp ring. Boullion will gather into a tight loop.

8. Pull needle and thread back through the 1st bead (nearest the clasp). Knot. Repeat for the next two beads.

9. Clip the short thread as close to the knot as possible and dab glue on the knot. Dab glue on 1st two knots (near clasp)

clip strings

glue

10. Knot the rest of the beads, leaving last three beads unknotted.

11. Thread on the second piece of boullion, looping thread and boullion through the clasp ring.

12. Pass thread back through 1st bead, knot. Then pass thread through 2nd and 3rd beads, knotting each.

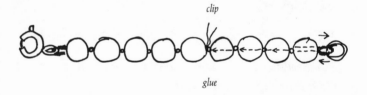

clip

glue

13. Pass thread back (without knots) through next 2 or 3 beads and cut thread very close.

14. Dab glue on cut, then sparingly on 1st three knots.

7" bracelet

Although this technique requires more time and skill than using a bead tip, it provides a very neat professional appearance and stronger closure. I recommend it for all fine pearls and beads.

5 STRINGING ON CHAIN

Some beads have extra large or sharp drill holes, and should be strung on Foxtail or cable linked chain. It is also preferable to string 14 Karat or Sterling beads on chain, for both security and appearance.

Foxtail is a flexible, smooth woven metal designed for heavy, large holed or sharp edged beads. It is available in four sizes, from very fine to heavy weight.

1. Measure chain two inches longer than anticipated length of necklace.

2. Using needle, pin, or small round file, open the hole in the last link.

3. Attach jump ring and clasp. (If jump ring is not to be soldered, it is wise to use a split ring).

4. String on all the beads.

5. Leaving ½"–¾" of chain extended from last bead, open the hole in link. Attach jump ring and clasp.

heavy metal pendant with stone and metal beads (on chain)

MORE SUGGESTIONS

1. Once you've mastered the technique of knotting, try experimenting with long and short spaces between beads, with different kinds of cords and with design innovation

2. Thread can enhance your design, with constrasting colors or multiple threads to match.

leather with wood beads closure

3. Make sure your cord and clasp will be strong enough to hold the weight of the beads.

assorted handmade metal closures

4. Always use the heaviest cord that can pass through the drill holes.

5. Experiment with wire, jump rings and a pair of pliers for variation. Necklaces, as well as bracelets and earrings can be made this way.

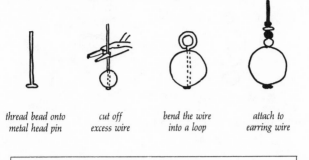

thread bead onto
metal head pin

cut off
excess wire

bend the wire
into a loop

attach to
earring wire

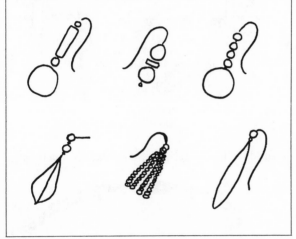

bead combinations

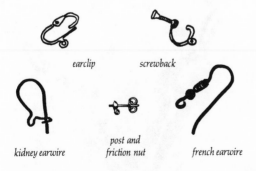

earclip
screwback

kidney earwire

post and
friction nut

french earwire

6. Commercial findings can be used for your bead designs.

7. Sometimes the use of wire for stringing beads can be very effective. Make wire loops to attach beads to each other, or to the clasp.

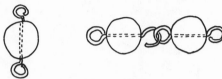

wire loops with beads

An adjustable closure can also be made this way.

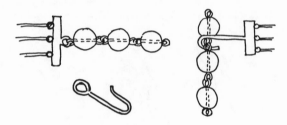

adjustable "chain" end

This same technique can be used to attach a pendant.

combining metal and beads

APPENDIX

STANDARD TERMINOLOGY
STANDARD MEASUREMENT
NUMBER OF BEADS NEEDED

4 strand lariat knotted at neck

attaching lariat or pendant

Standard Terminology

Beaded jewelry is generally described by standard terms and lengths. These measurements always include the clasp.

Bib: A necklace with three or more strands, with each one longer than the one above it.

Bracelet: A 7" length for the wrist.

Choker: Usually 16". A uniform necklace that drops to just above the collarbone.

Dog Collar: A necklace of three or more strands worn close on the neck.

Graduated: A necklace of gradually increasing size beads, with the smallest near the clasp, and the largest at the center.

Lariat: A necklace of 48" (or longer) that is not joined at the ends, but tied in a knot or wrapped around the neck.

Matinee: A necklace 20"–24" in length.

Opera: A necklace 28"–32" in length.

Princess: A necklace 18" in length.

Rope: A necklace 40"–45" or longer.

Uniform: A necklace of any length, with equal sized beads throughout.

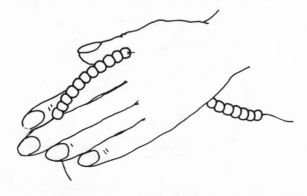

Standard Measurement

Beads are available in three forms:

Ball *Bead* *½ Drilled*
(Undrilled) *(Drilled Through)* *(For Pegsetting)*

Beads come in all shapes, materials and sizes, but they are almost always measured by millimeters (1/25 of an inch). Gemstone beads and pearls are sold in temporarily strung 16" lengths. The following measurements are very helpful in determining necessary supplies. (Some beads vary slightly.)

16" Temporarily Strung			
Size	**Beads**	**Size**	**Beads**
3mm	128	10mm	40
4mm	100	11mm	36
5mm	80	12mm	33
6mm	66	14mm	29
7mm	57	16mm	25
8mm	50	18mm	23
9mm	45	20mm	20

beads are measured from hole to hole

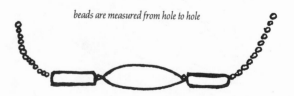

Number of Beads Needed

An easy way to determine how many beads you will need is to use the following formula:

$$1'' = 25.4mm$$

If your necklace is to be 15″, and you are using 6mm beads:

1. Multiply 25.4(mm) by 15 (inches).
$$25.4 \times 15 = 381 \text{ (mm)}$$

2. Divide 381 (mm) by 6 (mm).
$$381 \div 6 = 63.5 \text{ (beads)}$$

The result: 63.5 is the number of 6mm beads needed for a 15″ necklace. Since some beads may be of poor quality (poorly drilled, cracked or discolored), it is always wise to have a few extra beads on hand.

Subtract the width of spacers and clasp before stringing.

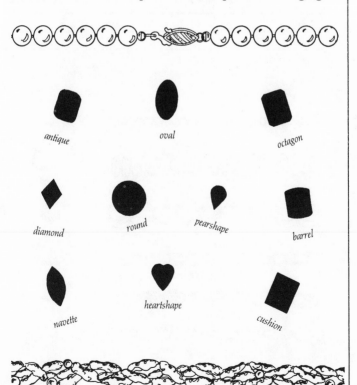

antique

oval

octagon

diamond

round

pearshape

barrel

navette

heartshape

cushion

Another way to figure how many beads are needed, is to use the following guide. (All figures have been rounded off and are approximate.)

Bead Size	Approximate Number of Beads Per Inch					
mm	1"	7"	16"	24"	32"	36"
3	8.25	57	132	200	265	288
4	6.25	43	100	150	200	225
5	5.00	35	82	124	160	180
6	4.25	28	67	100	132	153
7	3.50	24	57	85	114	126
8	3.25	22	50	75	100	112
9	2.75	19	45	67	90	101
10	2.50	18	40	60	80	90
12	2.00	15	33	50	66	72
14	1.75	13	29	43	56	63
16	1.50	11	25	38	50	54
18	1.25	10	23	34	45	45

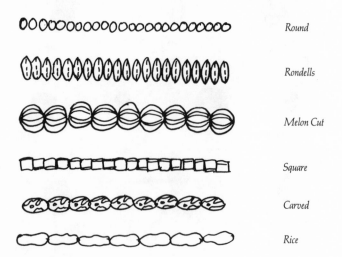

Round

Rondells

Melon Cut

Square

Carved

Rice

common bead shapes

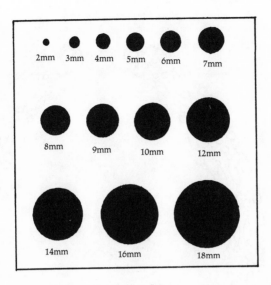

Exact (calibrated) Sizes

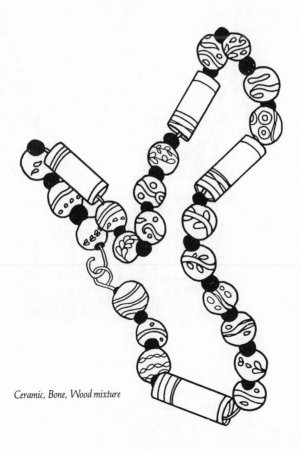

Ceramic, Bone, Wood mixture

Egyptian Collar

Museums are frequently a source of inspiration. Old beads and pendants can be found at estate sales, flea markets, and garage sales. Remember—original, well-crafted, beaded jewelry is unlimited.

NOTES